# New Zealand Country Wildlife

# WHICH? WHAT? WHY?

### Dave Gunson

**BATEMAN BOOKS**

## Why do swamps smell funny sometimes?

Because many swamps and wetlands have areas of stagnant (not flowing) water. Also, dead vegetation rots and decomposes, causing a build-up of gases — like hydrogen sulphide, which can smell a bit like rotten eggs (or even worse). Sometimes, a disturbance in the watery ground can cause a 'bubble' of gas to rise up and send a nasty stink wafting through the wetlands.

It's estimated that there were about 6700 square kilometres of wetlands in Aotearoa New Zealand before humans arrived and started 'improving' them. It's now down to 890 square kilometres — that's a loss of around 87 per cent.

## What makes the 'Boom! Boom!' noise in the wetlands at night?

That's the male Australasian bittern. This bird makes those loud booming noises to establish its territory, and to attract a mate. On a still night, the booming sound can be heard several kilometres away. The female bittern doesn't say very much, but she often 'burbles' to herself when she's around the nest. The bittern is a secretive bird, and, if disturbed, it will stretch upwards and 'freeze' — bill pointing to the sky — to try to disguise itself by blending in with its surroundings; it will even sway slightly, just as the reeds and raupō foliage around it move in the breeze.

## What's the difference between a lake and a pond?

It's a question of size — sort of. If a body of water is shallow enough for sunlight to penetrate to the bottom, which means that water plants are able to grow down there, it's a pond. If the body of water is too deep for sunlight to reach the bottom, and plants can't grow there, it's a lake. Of course, there are very small bodies of water that look like ponds that are deep enough to be called lakes, and huge bodies of shallow water that qualify as ponds, although because of their size, they might be called lakes.

IS THIS A POND OR A LAKE?

NAH, MATE. IT'S A POOL!

I THOUGHT IT WAS A LAGOON...

LOOKS MORE LIKE A BIG PUDDLE TO ME!

CREEK?

BROOK?

STREAM?

Our longest river is the Waikato, at 425 kilometres. All the rivers and major streams in New Zealand total about 425,000 kilometres in length — that's enough to reach to the moon (and go around it a few times, too!).

There are nearly 800 lakes in New Zealand. The largest is Lake Taupō, in the North Island, which covers 623 square kilometres. Lake Ellesmere, in the South Island, is 30 kilometres long but only 2 metres deep, so perhaps it should be called Ellesmere Pond — or perhaps Ellesmere Lagoon.

## Do kingfishers really catch fish?

Yes, they do. Kingfishers will usually find a perch on a tree branch that overlooks a stream or a lake, from where they can watch for the movement of small fish. They then dive straight into the water to scoop them up. They'll also watch mudflats for the movements of small crabs and insects, then fly down to snatch them up. A pair of kingfishers looking to make a nest will dig a tunnel in an earth bank by flying at it and digging with their heavy bills. Once a decent tunnel has been made, they build their nest inside.

The collective term for kingfishers is a 'realm' . . . but Mrs Gunson prefers a **dive** of kingfishers.

Another 'fishing' bird is the white-faced heron. It walks stealthily around waterways and then pauses to stir up the water with one foot to disturb and bring out fish, frogs and insects. The first of these birds arrived here from Australia in the early 1900s, and now it's the most common heron in New Zealand. It's happy to look for food away from waterways too, and will explore golf courses, orchards and even garden fishponds for a meal.

## Do ducks swim or paddle?

They don't need to swim to get about, as their big webbed feet make it easy to paddle along the surface of the water, *left-right-left-right* just like a diver with flippers on their feet. And when they come up on land, those big webbed feet mean that they walk awkwardly, again just like a diver with big flippers.

## Do ducks have nests like other birds?

Yes, they do. They usually make nests near water, often hidden in long grasses and shrubs. Any hidden place will do — sometimes they'll use a hole in the base of a tree, or even a quiet spot in the corner of someone's garden or in an old veggie plot.

The collective terms for ducks are a 'flock', a 'brace', a 'raft', a 'team' or a 'paddling' . . . but Mrs Gunson prefers a **waddle** of ducks.

## Do all ducks go 'quack'?

Some ducks say *quack*, but most ducks say something else. Some say *kraark* or *took-took-took*, while others say *whee* or just whistle, groan, cough, squeak or growl. It's usually the female duck that has a lot to say, while the male often stays almost silent.

## Why do ducks stick their bums in the air?

They're just looking for food when they do that. It's called 'dabbling'. Usually they're nibbling at water plants below the surface of the water or taking small water animals — such as insect larvae — from the water or the mud. Not all ducks feed this way; some prefer to skim along the water surface with their bills for small plants and insects.

## Are there any flowers that grow in the wetlands?

Yes, there are. The blue swamp orchid is one of the prettiest. New Zealand has over 80 species of native orchids, and they can grow in all sorts of situations — from the seashore to the mountains — and they appear in a wide range of colours. The blue swamp orchid is happy to grow in damp, boggy places.

## What's the bird that stands on rocks with its wings held out?

It's a species of shag. Shags can dive and chase after fish, eels and freshwater crayfish under the water. Their feathers are only partly waterproof, which means that there's no air layer to slow them down when they dive in the water. After a few dives, they need to stand and hold out their wings to let them dry off, as it's very difficult to fly properly with wet wings. They often nest in large groups in nearby trees. Shags are found all around the coast, or by lakes and rivers. Some like to dive in deep water, and some prefer to hunt in shallow water. They can travel quite a distance when submerged — propelled by their large, webbed feet — and stay under for a long time; sometimes for 2 to 3 minutes, although a normal dive is usually for about 40 seconds.

There are 12 species of shags in New Zealand, and about 36 known around the world, where they are more commonly called cormorants.

AW, MATE... YOU SHOULDA SEEN THE ONE THAT GOT AWAY... IT WAS *THIS BIG!*

## Can pūkeko make proper nests in the swamps?

Yes, they can. And they make some very big ones. Pūkeko mostly live in communal groups, and they build a large single nest, made from available reeds and raupō, hidden deep in the surrounding cover. It can be 30 centimetres or more high and can be so large that sometimes rough ramps need to be constructed to allow young birds to get in and out of the nest.

There can be anything from 8 to 15 birds in a group, male and female, and they all share the same territory and the same big nest. All the eggs are laid in this single nest — sometimes 15 eggs or more can be in the nest at the same time, and the birds all share in the care of the young.

Although they prefer plant food, pūkeko are happy to walk through the swamps to pick up food such as frogs, small fish and insects. They'll travel through pastures, roadside grass strips, gardens and parks to pick out plant shoots as well. They pluck the stalks and hold them up in one foot — parrot fashion — while they eat.

## Can pūkeko fly?

Yes, they can, but they're mostly reluctant flyers. They much prefer to walk about as they look for food. If they're disturbed, they usually run away and hide, rather than fly. Even though they lack webbed feet, as ducks have, they can also swim quite well.

## Do frogs really say 'ribbit'?

No, not really. There are several introduced frogs that live around the wetlands, and they make a strange collection of sounds. The whistling frog doesn't actually whistle but sounds more like a loud cricket. The southern bell frog (the longest frog at about 90 millimetres) doesn't sound like a bell — more like a rapid croaking. And the green and golden bell frog makes a sound rather like an ancient car horn that somebody stepped on!

New Zealand has three native frogs. All of them are small and rare. Two of them prefer damp forest situations away from wetlands, but the tiny Hochstetter's frog (about 45 millimetres in length) likes to be close to freshwater sites. It doesn't croak but makes a chirping noise instead.

## What do frogs eat?

A frog will take its prey with a quick flick of its long and very soft tongue, which is covered in a very sticky saliva. The tongue snaps back and, in one gulp, the victim is in the frog's throat and gone! Frogs will eat just about anything that moves within reach — crickets, moths, worms, flies, spiders.

The tongue is usually about one-third of the frog's body length. But as the tongue is attached to the front of the frog's mouth, instead of at the back — like our own tongues — it looks a lot longer when in action.

## How far can frogs jump?

Many can jump up to 20 times their own body length if fleeing danger, though small hops and leaps are usual for just getting about. Larger frogs overseas can make jumps of over 2 metres.

The collective term for frogs is an 'army' . . . but Mrs Gunson prefers a **croak** of frogs.

## What are those insects on the surface of the water?

There are lots of different insects that live on and around the surface of the water, and many have the strangest names. There's a tiny whirligig beetle, which spins about on the surface while it looks for prey below. Sometimes there can be crowds of these on the water, all spinning about without ever bumping into each other.

The water skater and the water measurer are so light and small that they can run about on the surface, while they search for tiny flying insects that may have become stuck in the water.

The waterboatman floats and uses its long legs as oars to move through the water to find small plants to feed on.

Strangest of all is the backswimmer. Like the waterboatman, it uses its legs as oars — but it floats about on its back! Its eyes are big enough to see down (or should that be 'up'?) into the water for prey such as tiny insect larvae and small crustaceans.

## What are the tiny dragonflies by lakes and streams called?

They're called damselflies. They're much smaller and daintier than their dragonfly cousins. There are about six species in New Zealand, in a variety of bright colours. Males and females are often seen in different shades and markings — blue, red, black, green and orange. The largest species — at a length of just 45 millimetres — is the blue damselfly.

They zip back and forth over water to snatch up small flying insects, and they will often chase off other damselflies who intrude on their own small 'territory', usually of just a few square metres.

When resting, damselflies fold their wings back together, but dragonflies rest with their wings held out.

There are about 1000 species of damselfly known around the world.

## Do mosquitoes bite, or do they sting?

They don't do either. They *pierce*. A mozzie's mouthparts are shaped into a sort of a sharp hollow needle, called a proboscis, which they use to poke through into another animal's skin and then draw blood. At the same time, the mozzie's saliva acts as a sort of lubricant for the proboscis and helps to thin the blood being sucked up. It's this saliva, not the 'bite', that causes the itch that we feel, as our immune system reacts to it. Only the female mosquito does this. Red blood is rich in the proteins that she needs to develop her eggs. Mosquitoes are drawn to humans and other animals — such as lizards and birds — by the carbon dioxide that we breathe out, as well as by the other chemicals and smells released by our skin.

They live and breed in any quiet water that isn't flowing, like small ponds — even in birdbaths, and any pools of water in grass patches, buckets or old tyres around houses. The young larvae, called 'wrigglers' (because they wriggle a lot!) develop in the water, where they can be prey for other insects, frogs and ducks.

SO, HOW COME YOU'RE FULL OF **BLUE** STUFF INSTEAD OF RED STUFF?

I MISSED DAVE'S FINGER AND STABBED A TUBE OF WATERCOLOUR PAINT INSTEAD!

It's not all a straightforward life for mosquitoes. There's actually a very tiny midge that will land on them and suck out some of the very blood that the mosquito has just taken from *us!*

The collective term for mosquitoes is a 'scourge' . . . but Mrs Gunson prefers a **nuisance** of mosquitoes.

## So what's the little black fly that bites?

It's a black fly! It's also called a sandfly and, like the mosquito, only the female sucks blood from other animals — usually penguins, seals and birds. There are 13 species in New Zealand, but only four will attack humans — and when they do, they often appear in annoyingly large swarms, especially around South Island coasts.

## Are the plants in lakes and rivers some kind of seaweed?

Yes . . . well, sort of. Seaweed is a general term for plants that live in water, but those in freshwater like lakes and rivers are more properly called algae (and sometimes called 'pondweeds'). Many float on the lake or stream surface, and some have roots that hang down to draw nutrients from the water. Sometimes they can form large mats or rafts, where animals such as frogs, insects and spiders can rest or keep a closer watch on the water for a possible feed. And underneath, other creatures hide. There are many plants that like to have 'wet feet' too, with proper roots in the beds and banks of streams, and others — such as raupō and reed species — further out into the boggy grounds of nearby marshes and swamps.

There are plenty of small plants, too. The sundew, with its pretty little flowers, is actually a killer. If an insect lands on a leaf and gets stuck in the goo on its sticky hair-like tentacles, it starts a chemical reaction and the other tentacles bend inwards — to trap, kill and then digest the trapped insect. When 'lunch' has been absorbed, the tentacles all open out again, to wait for the next unsuspecting visitor.

OOOH, WHAT A PRETTY LITTLE LEAF...

The sundew isn't our only 'carnivorous' plant. In the wetlands' muddy grounds, the tiny bladderwort waits for small insects to inspect its flowers and leaves. It has small bladder-like pods — traps — attached to its stems. If an insect brushes against tiny 'trigger' hairs on the leaf, the trap snaps open and the prey is swept inside.

There are about 500 species of animal-eating plants around the world, and some are large enough to trap larger insects, lizards and frogs.

### Are there any shellfish or crabs in rivers and lakes, like at the seaside?

Yes. There are quite a few small shellfish, such as mussels, snails and limpets. There are shrimps and a little freshwater crab that measures only about 10 millimetres across the back. There are crayfish, too. New Zealand has two species of freshwater crayfish or kōura. At about 16 centimetres in length, they're much smaller than the crayfish in the seas, but they have something their big cousins don't have — large pincers!

These crayfish hide in sandy stream beds or behind rocks during the day, then come out at night to feed on plant material and small water animals. They'll usually run off backwards if disturbed by predators such as eels and large fish (and human fishers), but, if cornered, they'll use their pincers to defend themselves.

One oddity to be found in rocky streams in the North Island is the 11-millimetre-long black limpet. It looks like a mini version of a pāua shell, and it lives attached to the undersides of stones. Just like its seashore cousins, it roams around the rocks to scrape algal growths and then returns to its home 'spot'.

The oddity is that it's the only freshwater limpet species in the world to emit bioluminescence — it creates its own light, just like a glow-worm. If disturbed, it will slide away and leave behind a glowing green slime to distract any predator.

### Are freshwater eels dangerous?

Well, you don't want to mess with them too much — they have lots of small, sharp teeth. If you're wading in a shallow stream, an eel might like to investigate your toes! But, generally, eels will avoid trouble.

They usually rest during the day and are active in the evening when they swim about looking for something to eat — snails, freshwater crayfish, insects and fish . . . if you drop your picnic lunch in the stream, they'll probably pinch that as well.

New Zealand has two species — the long-finned eel and the short-finned eel. The long-finned eel is the larger of the two, and it's the longest of all the world's freshwater eels. Though most are about 1.2 metres in length, some very large specimens can measure nearly 2 metres and weigh up to 50 kilograms.

Eels are found throughout most of New Zealand's freshwater habitats — and they can even wriggle and slide their way across wet ground to move from one stream to another. These eels move to the sea and then travel over 2000 kilometres into the Pacific Ocean to spawn and lay eggs before they die (a female long-finned eel can lay up to 20 million tiny eggs). The resulting tiny eels eventually find their way back to New Zealand's rivers, and continue to grow slowly to adulthood here.

### So, are eels fish, or what?

Yes, they're fish. Although they're slimy and snake-like, they have gills, fins and scales just like 'proper' fish.

Eels usually live in New Zealand waters for 20 to 40 years, before returning to the ocean to reproduce, but some remain — one long-finned eel studied at Lake Rotoiti in Nelson Lakes National Park was found to be about 106 years old!

## Do you get cabbages from cabbage trees?

Yes, of course. *Just kidding*! They're only called cabbage trees because the new shoots — when cooked by early European arrivals (including Captain Cook's crew) — tasted a bit like cabbage or artichoke. They also made beer from the roots. The plant is called tī or tī kōuka by Māori, who also cooked the leaf bud, taproots and stems for a range of food and medicinal preparations. Different parts of the tree were used to make sandals, baskets, capes, ropes and for roof thatching. The berries are a favourite food for many birds, especially kererū.

It's a very tough and hardy tree, which grows throughout the country. It can live for 200 to 800 years.

## What's that little lizard sitting on a rock?

That's probably a skink. These small lizards mostly prefer to live in open and high country, where they can hide easily in vegetation or around rocky ground but can come out quickly to bask motionless on warm rocks in the sun. They'll take insects, spiders and some small fruits to eat. They're quite small animals — usually measuring around 12 to 20 centimetres, measured from tail tip to nose — although some larger species can reach up to 35 centimetres.

If attacked, the skink can detach its tail, which will then writhe and thrash for a while to distract the predator, while the skink makes a quick escape. The skink will then slowly grow a new tail, which is usually a bit smaller than the original.

Geckos can shed their tails this way, too.

Lizards are probably the most successful type of reptile — they evolved about 300 million years ago. There are over 11,000 reptile species known around the world, and nearly 2000 of them are skinks. New Zealand has about 50 native species.

### What's the little owl that perches on fenceposts?

The little owl that perches on fenceposts is called the little owl — mostly because — at a length of just 23 centimetres — it really *is* a little owl (marvellous how they come up with these clever names, isn't it?). It's also known as the German owl or brown owl. It was introduced here over 100 years ago, to help keep the numbers of sparrows and finches down, as they were causing problems on farms. But it turned out that the owl much preferred to eat worms, spiders and insects.

Unlike most other owls, it prefers to hunt and fly in the daytime, which is why it's often seen keeping watch for prey from the top of posts and hedges. If it sees anything interesting, it will fly to the ground and run about to seek out food.

It will bob up and down, and rotate its head, if it's disturbed, as it tries to assess the threat.

## What's the big bird that swoops down and snatches up dead animals off the road?

That's the Australasian harrier or swamp harrier. It hunts for food, such as lizards, rats and rabbits, by flying and circling over open country and forest edges. When it sees a likely lunch, it swoops down to chase and catch the victim in its large claws.

Of course, it's much easier to simply fly down and grab an animal that's already been killed, like possums or hedgehogs run over by traffic on the road. Harriers can often be seen pecking at some roadkill, then flying to the side of the road when a car comes past and returning to their meal when the road's quiet again. Young harriers develop their skills by jumping and pouncing at rats and insects on the ground. Some adult harriers can measure around 60 centimetres in length and weigh about 850 grams. They can live for around 18 years.

One of New Zealand's other birds of prey is the falcon — kārearea — which is only about half the size of the harrier but much more aggressive. It will attack other birds in flight — tūī, magpie and kererū, for example — and will even take on the harrier. The falcon usually selects a high perch, from where it can spot small animals on the ground, and it can swoop down on them at speeds of up to 180 kilometres an hour. Falcons can live for about 6 to 10 years.

## What are those tall, white feathery plants called?

They're called toetoe. They're actually New Zealand's tallest-growing native grass and can reach up to 3 metres in height. Māori used this plant's leaves to make mats and baskets, and they used it in wall linings and roof thatching. It's also called 'cutty grass' because the saw-like edges to the leaves can cut the skin.

There's a form of this grass called pampas, which was introduced from South America. Pampas spreads very easily and smothers other plants, so it's now regarded as an invasive plant — a country-wide 'weed'. Toetoe produces its tall, drooping white-yellowish flowerheads around springtime, while pampas flowers in mid-to-late summer, and its upright flowers are a dull pink-purple, which later fade to a dirty white. Some native toetoe can also appear in pinkish forms, too — so it can be hard to tell the difference sometimes!

## And what about those tall colourful plants seen in the South Island?

They're lupins, and they're mostly seen around the Mackenzie Country. They're very pretty to look at, especially when there are hillsides and fields full of them, and they make a great food for sheep — they love to eat the flowers and the leaves. But lupins are also seen as an invasive weed; they can spread to the banks of waterways and become so crowded that there's hardly any room for birds — like the black stilt — to use their usual nesting grounds.

## What makes the little holes in clay banks and bare earth?

They're probably the homes of the tiger beetle grubs (or 'penny doctors'). The tunnels are around 15 centimetres deep and the grubs live in them for about a year. They will grab and eat any small insect that happens to pass by the burrow entrance. The adult tiger beetle, 1 centimetre long, can be seen on open ground throughout the country, running about almost non-stop and making short flights, as it seeks out insects to catch with its large, barbed jaws. At night, the beetle digs itself in under the ground and then emerges the next morning. There are about 12 species of tiger beetle in New Zealand, and about 2600 are known around the world.

Tiger beetles and cockroaches are the fastest-running insects. A species of Australian tiger beetle can run at 2.5 kilometres per hour — that's about equal to the speed of a human 'stroll' . . . which is a very impressive speed for a tiny insect.

## So what about the other holes in the ground?

They might be the homes of trapdoor spiders, though they're harder to see. They construct burrows in the earth — sometimes up to 30 centimetres deep — lined with silk, and they also make hinged and tightly fitting 'lids' out of silk. They wait just inside the entrance, with the lid slightly open. When they detect the motion of a passing insect, they dash out to grab the victim and drag it back down into the burrow. They're some of our most robust and strongest spiders, with body lengths of up to 3 centimetres, and they can live for about 20 years.

New Zealand has about 40 species of trapdoor spiders, with about 260 species known around the world.

## How high can insects fly?

Because they're so lightweight, winged insects are often at the mercy of wind currents when they fly very high — butterflies have been seen flying at 6000 metres, partly by their own efforts, and with plenty of 'help' from rising winds. Most insects are comfortable flying within heights of 10 to 20 metres — the smaller the insect, the closer to the ground it will fly. Winged insects have either a single pair of wings, as with mosquitoes and house flies, but most have two pairs, like bees, dragonflies, cicadas, moths and butterflies.

## Can insects fly as fast as birds?

Yes — some are more than capable of keeping up with the normal bird flight speeds of between 25 and 50 kilometres per hour. Dragonflies can get to nearly 60 kilometres an hour, in top gear! And with their four wings capable of being moved independently, they can turn, swoop, hover and go up or down as fast as they like.

Small flies, like midges, can flap their wings 60,000 times a minute, while a monarch butterfly might flap less than 500 times.

## How many legs do insects have?

Insects have six legs. Sometimes the front pair of legs are specially adapted for uses other than walking, climbing or running; they often have claws or extra joints to allow the insect to hold objects or to grasp or trap prey. There can be special adaptations — for example, some butterflies have very small front legs, which they can use to detect smell and taste, and the wētā's 'ears' are located just below the knee joints of its front legs.

Other adaptations include having longer back legs for jumping, such as wētā, crickets and grasshoppers have. Some water insects have legs that they can use as oars (see page 9), and the praying mantis has an extra spike to its long, folded front legs, to impale or trap prey.

HEY DAD... WHADDYA RECKON?

The word 'insect' comes from the Latin word *insectum* — which means 'with a divided body'. All insects have three body parts: the head, with eyes, antennae and mouth parts; the thorax (the middle part) with all the muscles required for the legs and wings; and at the rear the abdomen, which contains the heart, digestive and reproductive organs . . . and sometimes a weapon, in the form of a venomous sting!

## Can stick insects fly?

No, New Zealand species of stick insect can't fly. They all have to walk — and often they walk in a very wobbly and hesitant fashion, as they climb through the branches of their favourite food plants, usually mānuka and kānuka. They're found in forest and forest fringes, and out in more open country. There's even one species which prefers to live in alpine tussock.

Our range of species are coloured in shades of grey-brown, brown or green, and either smooth, knobbly or prickly. The largest species can be 15 to 20 centimetres in length, and the smallest are just 4 to 5 centimetres.

During the day, they rest — pressed against a twig or branch — with front legs extended, and they are almost impossible to spot. The most common stick insect in New Zealand is — *wait for it* — the common stick insect!

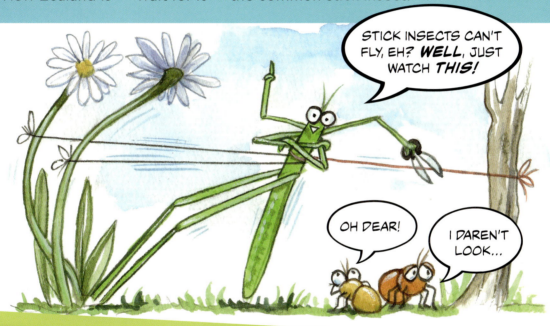

There are stick insect species overseas that can fly, and there are species that have wings but cannot fly. Some are known as 'leaf insects' as they have body extensions that make them look just like — yes, you guessed it — a leaf. There are about 3000 species known worldwide.

The longest stick insects in the world can measure around 60 centimetres or more, with the front legs stretched out in their normal position. That's about the same measurement as the two-page spread — plus *one more page* — of this book that you're holding!

## Why do tūī like flax flowers?

It's the nectar in the flowers that they're after. Tūī have a sort of 'brush' ending to their long tongues, and they can take up quite a lot of nectar. They also like the nectar from other flowers such as those of kōwhai and rewarewa, and they'll often chase off other birds from their favourite plants. When they push their long bills into the flowers, they get pollen on their heads, which helps to pollinate the plants as they move from place to place. If there's no nectar to be found, tūī are quite happy to change their diet and hunt larger insects, such as cicadas or stick insects.

There are two types of flax (harakeke) in New Zealand — common flax and mountain flax. Common flax grows up to 3 metres high, with flower stalks up to about 4 metres, with seedpods that stand erect, while mountain flax rarely grows more than 1.6 metres high, and the pods hang down. There are many varieties of flax, with a range of flower colours — from yellow to orange and shades of red.

Other 'brush-tongue' birds include the bellbird, stitchbird and the silvereye. All are happy to collect the nectar from a wide variety of flowers. Bird tongues are usually rounded or slightly triangular in section, and smooth. The 'brush' is simply a sort of 'frayed brush' ending to the tongue's tip — and different species of birds can have differently shaped 'brushes'.

European settlers referred to the plant as flax because of the similarities of its plant fibres to those of flax overseas — our 'flax' is actually a form of lily.

## Do all flowers have nectar in them?

All the plants that need insects or birds to carry pollen from plant to plant (most plants need a 'mix' of pollen before they can reproduce) will have flowers with sweet nectar to attract visitors. Birds and insects — bees, for example — will get brushed with pollen as they enter the flower, and then this will get distributed as they visit, and then pollinate, other plants of the same type. The plants can then produce fruit and seeds to create new offspring.

Favourite nectar plants include flax, kōwhai, cabbage tree, mānuka — all will attract plenty of pollinating visitors.

## Is tussock just some sort of giant grass?

Yes, it is. There are many different tussocks in New Zealand, and they can be found growing throughout the country, in all sorts of environments — from the coast to high in the mountains, although 'upland country' is the most favoured. Some may measure less than half a metre in height, but many can grow to heights of 2 metres of more, and they can appear in a wide range of colours — brown, red, gold, red-brown . . . and green, of course. Some of the hardier types can live for up to 300 years.

Tussock is not just one species of grass, but simply a range of hardy grasses that have a similar growth pattern — to form growing tufts or clumps. And swathes of these clumps across the land provide shelter, protection and food for others — smaller plants are shielded from the worst of the weather, and the range of animals living in and around tussock is remarkable; there are all kinds of insects, lizards and birds.

There are about 190 native grass species, and most have a tussock form of growth. Although grass might seem to be a 'primitive' form of plant, it was actually one of the last major plant types to evolve — just before the end of the dinosaurs, about 65 million years ago.

## Did the grasshopper get its name just because it hops about on the grass?

Yes. New Zealand has about 15 species of grasshopper (with short antennae), and many are only found in certain parts of the country. Some have wings and some don't. The green katydid is a form of grasshopper (with long antennae), and it can often be seen in gardens.

Closely related is the black field cricket — often seen in gardens, too, or jumping and running across the carpet in the lounge!

## Which bird is it that sings high up in the sky in the country?

That'll be a skylark. Early European settlers missed this bird's pretty song, so they brought it here in the 1860s. It seems that there are now more skylarks in Aotearoa New Zealand than there are in England. In spring, the skylark will fly high up into the sky, singing sweetly as it rises and then circles about. It feeds on the ground, looking for insects, spiders and seeds. Skylarks often like to take dust baths on the dry grounds by country roads, and when they need a wash, they'll crouch or lie down out in the rain with both wings fully extended.

## What are the little yellow birds hopping about on the ground?

They're called yellowhammers. Like the skylark, they were brought here from England in the 1860s and are now found throughout the country. They're similar in size to the skylark, too — about 16 to 18 centimetres in length. They nest close to the ground, rather than high up in trees, and they hop and walk about to look for food on the open ground, such as seeds, insects, grubs and spiders. They can sometimes be seen in large flocks of 100 to 300 birds. The yellowhammer's song — *tintintintintink-swee* — has often been written down as 'a little bit of bread and no cheese'.

## Is the kea really some kind of parrot?

Yes, it is. No other parrot in the world lives at such high altitudes as the kea. They're very happy in the mountains and even in the snow. They're very smart birds, and experiments have shown that they're quite capable of solving mazes and complex puzzles. They have quite a reputation for being inquisitive, and they'll investigate any object they find — to play with it, take it to pieces or even steal it, if they can!

Initially considered to be a danger to sheep by early European settlers, thousands of kea were killed, but they have been a protected bird since 1986. They're named after their call of *kee-aa*.

Kea usually feed on a range of insects, seeds and fruits, but they will also take carrion (dead animals) and any food that humans might leave unattended. They can weigh up to a kilogram, with a length of about 46 centimetres. They can live for 15 to 20 years.

THIS IS GREAT! A FEW MORE TRIPS AND WE'LL BE ABLE TO BUILD OUR OWN TOYOTA COROLLA!

The correct terms for a group of parrots are a 'prattle', a 'company' or a 'pandemonium', and Mrs Gunson thinks the last one sounds about right.

## Are there lizards in the mountains?

Yes, there are quite a few living up there. There are several species of skinks and geckos that are either so secretive or rare that some have only been seen once or twice. In Otago's alpine zone, there's an unusual grey gecko with brown markings and bright orange spots. Experts reckon that there are about 17 alpine-dwelling skinks and 13 gecko species, out of our total count of 106 lizard species.

One remarkable alpine lizard is the black-eyed gecko — also known as Whitaker's sticky-toed gecko. It lives at the highest altitude of any lizard in New Zealand, up to 2200 metres above sea level in the South Island's Southern Alps — that's almost as high as Mt Ngāuruhoe in the North Island (or nearly seven times the height of the Auckland Sky Tower!).

It's of average gecko size (up to about 90 millimetres, not including the tail) with patterned grey skin, but its eyes are unique — instead of having a pale, patterned iris, as other geckos have — its iris is completely black.

Like many geckos, it has a colourful mouth — a pink or orange interior, with a pink or orange tongue.

*LOOKS COOL, THOUGH...*

*YOU STILL DON'T LOOK LIKE A BLACK-EYED GECKO, HARRY...*

Two of our largest lizards live in high country in the South Island — the Otago skink and the grand skink. They can reach lengths of 30 centimetres, measured from snout to tail tip. Both have very dramatic markings — the grand skink is black with yellow patches, and the Otago skink is black with yellow, green or grey patches. The colours and markings make for great camouflage among the rocks, lichens and plants. They can both live for about 20 years.

## Do any wētā live high up in the mountains?

Yes, they do. Giant wētā were once common throughout New Zealand, but they are now restricted to pest-free offshore islands, with the exception of the giant wētā still to be found high in the mountains. Large populations have survived up there, as such high altitudes are unpleasant for predators such as rats.

There are a number of species, and the most common is the giant wētā that lives on and around the scree (loose stones) slopes of the Southern Alps — and it's called . . . *yes*, the scree wētā! It's not quite a *giant* giant wētā — although some female scree wētā can have a body length of over 7 centimetres — that honour goes to the giant wētā on protected offshore islands, who can measure 10 centimetres or more.

The scree wētā often appears in colours to blend in with its immediate surroundings and make it harder to see. They may be grey, brown, red, olive or near-black — or even a mix of colours.

The scree wētā generally rests and hides during the day under the jumble of rocks and stones, and then emerges in the evening to feed on small plants and lichens . . . and the occasional small insect.

In captivity, this wētā will happily dine on lettuce, clover, fruit, carrots . . . and even a nice bit of cheese, too.

There is another significant wētā that lives in the alpine zone — a tiny black cave wētā, just 14 to 20 millimetres in body length, that hides in cracks in the rocks. When the weather is warm, it comes out to feed, and being such an agile jumper, climbers have referred to it as the Mount Cook Flea!

## Are there any butterflies in the mountains?

Yes, lots. There are probably more types of butterflies in higher places — especially in tussock country — than there are in forests and open country. Most higher country butterflies are orange-coloured, brown or dark brown, and some have 'eye spots' on their wings, to scare predators. One of the most common is the orange and black (and aptly named) common copper butterfly, which can also be seen in all sorts of environments — from mountains all the way down to the coast.

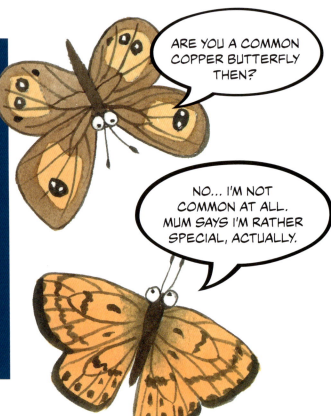

ARE YOU A COMMON COPPER BUTTERFLY THEN?

NO... I'M NOT COMMON AT ALL. MUM SAYS I'M RATHER SPECIAL, ACTUALLY.

GOOD EVENING, MORNING.

GOOD MORNING, EVENING.

New Zealand has at least 20 butterfly species, but probably more than 2000 species of moths. Most moths fly in the evenings and rest during the day, but some — like the black and white magpie moth — fly in the daytime, and rest at night, as most butterflies do. But then, some butterflies like to rest in the day, and fly about in the evening — like many high-country ringlet butterflies . . .

## Why aren't there any forests in the mountains?

It's all to do with a thing called the tree line. Larger plants (yes, trees are just 'larger plants') find it difficult to grow in the harsher and colder environments of higher regions in the country, and there comes a point where it's just too high for any tree to grow. This is the tree line.

And this is generally where the alpine zone begins, and some distance above this is where the snow is on the ground all year long.

There are still many plants — hardy shrubs and flowering plants — that can grow and thrive in the harsh conditions above the tree line.

The collective term for flowers is a 'bunch', a 'posy', a 'bouquet', a 'spray', a 'corsage', a 'boutonnière' or a 'nosegay' . . . but Mrs Gunson prefers 'These flowers are for *you*, darling.'

There are buttercups and daisies in the mountain slopes and valleys, but not like the ones in your garden. The Mount Cook lily is actually a close relative of the garden buttercup, and it is probably the largest buttercup in the world. It bears huge white flowers about 10 centimetres across, and the plant has leaves the size of a man's hand! This giant can grow to 1.5 metres in height and can survive in the alpine zone for 20 to 50 years.

There are about 50 species of mountain daisies. And they're giants, too — they can also have flowers 10 centimetres wide.

There are heaps of other plants that do well in the higher countryside — hebe, foxglove, gentian, orchids, tussock grasses (page 23) and vegetable sheep (page 30).

## Is the vegetable sheep a vegetable or a sheep?

It's a vegetable — or, more correctly, it's called a cushion plant. Several kinds of these plants can be found growing in higher altitudes. They have very densely packed branches with lots of tiny pale flowers and woolly leaves. They can grow to 60 centimetres or higher and a couple of metres across. From a distance, a group of them can appear as a flock of sheep resting on the ground. Some stories tell of newly arrived Europeans in the 1800s, whose sheepdogs were so confused by the plants that they tried to run around them and herd the 'sheep' together.

## Takahē have big wings, so why can't they fly?

Yes, they do have wings, but they're just not large enough to get the birds into the air, as takahē have evolved to become solidly built ground-dwelling creatures, with denser bones than flying birds. They can weigh up to 4 kilograms and measure about 63 centimetres in length. They use their wings mostly to 'show off' when mating, or when they argue and fight. They're very protective of their territory, and they'll even rush and attack human intruders during the breeding season. Their bills are heavy and strong — and sharp enough to chop and eat tussock and fern bases . . . and take the end off an enquiring human finger if they're annoyed. When takahē run about, they might flap their wings a lot, but they can never manage to actually take off.

## Are there mountain goats in New Zealand?

Yes, lots. The very first goats were released in the Marlborough Sounds in 1773 by Captain Cook, and since then there have been several species of deer and goats released into New Zealand — there was even a small population of moose released in Fiordland, but none have been seen for many years.

There are many 'ordinary' goats that have become feral (wild), and there are thousands of Himalayan tahr (a relative of goats and sheep) throughout the rocky slopes of the Southern Alps. All these species are seen as pests, as they browse on and destroy important native vegetation.

Goats are close relatives of sheep, and while they have many similarities, one difference is that while sheep say *baaa*, goats just say . . . *meh*.

## Do any birds live up in the alpine zone?

Rock wrens are our only true alpine birds, as they spend their whole lives above the tree line, in the South Island. These tiny birds — just 10 centimetres in length — live rather like small mice among the rocks very high up in the mountains. They scurry about and poke under the stones of mountain slopes to find spiders and insects — such as beetles — to eat. Although they can fly, they'd rather hop, skip and run as they move about, with just the occasional short-distance flutter to get from place to place. They can survive alpine winters by finding small spaces and crevices under rocks, where they can shelter from the harsh weather. They can live for up to 8 years.

Text © Dave Gunson, 2021
Typographical design © David Bateman Ltd, 2021

Published in 2021 by David Bateman Ltd
Unit 2/5 Workspace Drive, Hobsonville, Auckland 0618, New Zealand
www.batemanbooks.co.nz

ISBN 978-1-98-853888-4

This book is copyright. Except for the purpose of fair review, no part may be stored or transmitted in any form or by any means, electronic or mechanical, including recording or storage in any information retrieval systems, without permission in writing from the publisher. No reproduction may be made, whether by photocopying or by any other means, unless a licence has been obtained from the publisher or its agent.

The author asserts his moral right to be identified as author of this work.

Illustrations: Dave Gunson
Book design: Alice Bell and Dave Gunson
Printed in China by Toppan Leefung Printing Ltd